Born to Shop®

Born to Shop®

In Praise of the Modern Woman

PRION

This is a Prion book

First published in Great Britain in 2006 by Prion
An imprint of the Carlton Publishing Group
20 Mortimer Street
London W1T 3JW

Born to Shop © and ® 2006 History and Heraldry Ltd

10-digit ISBN: 1-85375-609-1

13-digit ISBN: 9-781-85375-609-2

Printed in Singapore

Contents

Born to be Beautiful

Lord if you won't make me skinny, please make my friends fat

I keep trying to lose weight, but it keeps finding me

Whenever I get the urge to exercise, I lie down until the feeling passes

Warning: This person may contain coarse language, and occasional scenes of nudity

I am usually gorgeous,
but it's my day off

At my age a soak
in the tub is just a
wild night in

You can't control
everything, your hair
was put on your head to
remind you of that

Born to be the
Model Partner

Sometimes I wake up grumpy, and sometimes I let him sleep

I don't do mornings

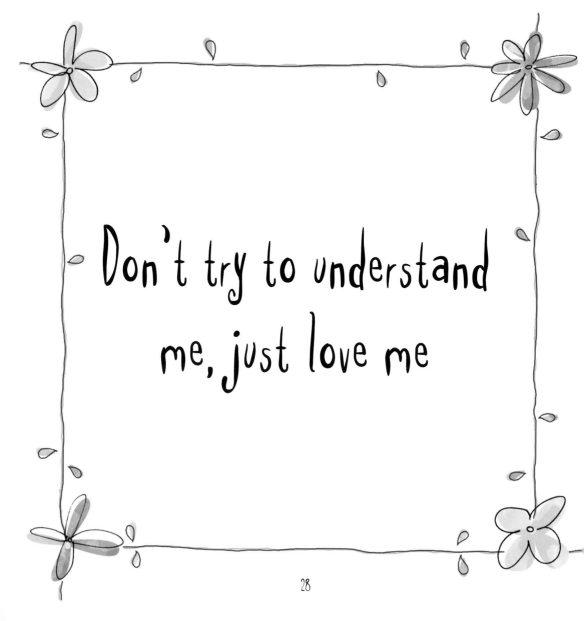

Don't try to understand me, just love me

I'm in my own world.
It's ok, they know
me here

If at first you
don't succeed,
try it your wife's way

All men are created equal, equally useless

When I married
Mr Right, I didn't
know his first name
was always

Laugh, and the world
laughs with you...
...snore and you sleep alone

Would you like to speak to the man in charge or the woman who knows what's happening

When I said
'I do', I didn't
mean everything

B.B.Q. — (bar-by-que) —

compact home incinerator used for disposing of bulky pieces of meat and poultry

A real man can barbie
any time, anywhere

I can only please one
person per day.
Today is not your day.
Tomorrow doesn't look
very good either

Three things real men
can't say, I'm wrong,
I'm lost, I can't fix it

I want a man who's kind
and understanding.
Is that too much to ask
of a millionaire?

Born to Eat What you Can

A balanced diet is a burger in each hand

Never eat more than
you can lift

Save the Earth,
it's the only planet
with chocolate

There's nothing better than a good friend except a good friend with chocolate

At Easter, size does count

So much chocolate
log, so little time

Born to be a
Yummy Mummy

We child proofed the house, but they keep finding their way in

Welcome to
Grandma's house.
Children spoilt
while you wait

Mothers of little
boys work from son
up to son down

'M' is for Mother, not for Maid

If a mother's place is in the home, why am I always in the car!

Born to be Wild

Seen it all, done it all, can't remember most of it

One tequila,
two tequila, three
tequila, floor!

I'm on a gin and
tonic diet, so far I've
lost two days

Life's too short to drink bad wine

The whole world is about three drinks behind

Born to be a Domestic Goddess

I kiss better than I cook

I love to cook with wine,
sometimes I even put it
in the food

Tis the season to be jolly

It's all too much, wake
me when it's over

Too much of a good
thing is wonderful

I am woman
I am invincible
I am tired

You can touch the
dust, but please
don't write in it

Many people have eaten in this kitchen and have gone on to live normal healthy lives

If you want breakfast in bed,
sleep in the kitchen

We eat all the main food groups — microwave, fast and frozen

If you want the best
seat in the house,
you'll have to move
the cat

People who don't like
cats must have been
mice in a previous life

Love endures all things

Born to Succeed

No coffee, no workee

We may not have it
all together...
but together we
have it all

Hard work pays off
in the future, laziness
pays off now

Instant human,
just add bubbles

This life must be a test,
if it were the real thing we'd
be given better instructions

I don't suffer from stress, but I am a carrier

Good morning...
let the stress begin

Born to be Part of the Gang

You can't have
too many friends,
or pairs of shoes

friends like you
don't grow on trees
I know this is true,
but if friends were flowers
there is no doubt how
quickly I'd pick you

For listening and caring and giving and sharing, for always being there thank you

Precious and few are

friends like you

A hug is a great
gift one size
fits all

148

Friends are the family we
choose for ourselves

There are special people
who touch our lives in a
certain way and having
known them we will never
be the same again

I can't imagine in
all the world a better
friend than you

Today I stopped and thought, what a special friend I have in you

Friends bring out the beautiful things in each other that nobody else looks hard enough to find

You'll always be my friend, you know too much